How to be a
UGANDAN

Joachim Buwembo

Fountain Publishers

Fountain Publishers Ltd
P.O. Box 488
Kampala
E-mail:fountain@starcom.co.ug
Website:www.fountainpublishers.com

ISBN 9970 02 379 9

Illustrations by Dan Barongo

————————————

Cataloguing-in-Publication Data

Buwembo, Joachim
    How to be a Ugandan/ Joachim Buwembo. – Kampala
Fountain Publishers, 2002
        p.; ill.; cm.

ISBN 9970 02 379 9

1. Humour - Uganda. I. Satire II. Title

808.796761 BUW

Dedication

This book is written in honour of all members of the Ugandan press, living and departed, who have over the years kept the world informed of the developments in our country.

Contents

Introduction

When veteran journalist and publisher James Tumusiime first suggested that I apply my style of writing to broader and more enduring issues on the country which could be published in book form, I wanted to disqualify myself. For despite having written numerous newspaper stories and commentaries, I was not sure I knew how books are written.

Even now after putting the last full stop on *How To Be a Ugandan*, I cannot say that I know how normal books are written. However, this is not a normal book in the sense that a sociologist would have presented it. And James assured me that I did not have to think too hard; all I had to do was to tell the people my perceptions as a journalist, of the other side of the Ugandan society, much the same way I normally do in short commentaries. I accepted the challenge and the result is *How To Be a Ugandan*.

The work was difficult, but finally, I did my part. Other observers of our society can also have their say. This is just a one-man's view of that other type of Ugandan, who is rarely talked or written about, but who is always present and whose qualities in all aspects of the nation's life have regrettably come to be accepted as the norm.

After reading this little book, I only invite you to ask yourself one question: Does the type of Ugandan portrayed constitute the majority or the minority of our society? If this Ugandan ever becomes the minority, Uganda will be a much better place to live in!

Joachim Buwembo
October 2002
Kampala

██●██ Businessman

A Ugandan enters and leaves business the same way - mysteriously. At any given time there is a business fad. It may be a fast-food takeaway restaurant, vegetable export, coffee smuggling, fish processing or stationery import. One day you know a man as a hospital clerk, the next day he is a stationery importer. Then one day, without warning, he is out of the stationery business, and has a long story about ruthless tax regimes, diabolical Indian traders and a non-supportive government.

Although the life history of a Ugandan businessman is mysterious, it is fairly simple, and short. There are two types of businessmen, the small- and the big-timer. The small-timer may be of any age. A long-serving senior civil servant attains the official retirement age of fifty-five and is forced to retire. He gets his terminal benefits amounting to about $20,000. With bulging pockets, he descends onto Kampala's commodity trading hub called Kikuubo. He tells whoever cares to hear that he resigned because he was tired of being exploited by government and he now wants to do his own thing.

At 55, our civil servant is reluctant to learn the essential tricks that are best performed by people in their early twenties – dodging the tax authorities, adulterating cooking oil, diluting bottled juice and playing one supplier off against another. His sales are almost nil as he cannot match the streetwise competitors and he is soon squeezed out – simple. Not that the twenty-something trader who buys out our retired civil servant will last much longer in the shop, or stall, to be more precise. He will remain in Kikuubo all right, but not as a stall owner. With no corporate culture, his personal life and business operations are one and the same. This is one mix that does not last.

On buying the stall, our small-time trader declares to those close to him that he has arrived in the big league. After years as a small-time broker in Kikuubo – one who grabs customers and directs them to the shop that has what they want in return for a commission from the shop owner – he now sets up shop as a cement dealer. Though very expensive in Uganda compared to other countries, cement is a fast selling commodity because of the perpetual construction boom, with everybody trying to become a house owner.

Using all his savings and a few loans from individuals, our man buys ten tonnes of cement in 200 bags of 50 kilos each. With the proceeds from selling the first tonne, he pays rent for his small residence. Cash from selling the second tonne goes to paying his son's school fees. With cash from the third tonne he buys food and other provisions at the house. Money from the fourth tonne is for paying rent for that elusive girlfriend he had lost to a more prosperous trader. He buys her shoes and a

makeup kit as well to make sure she remains his – for a while. Cash from the fifth tonne is used to buy South African food supplements for his terminally sick aunt. The sixth and seventh tonnes are used to finance an extravagant last funeral rites feast for his dead father. This earns him a lot of respect in the clan, as elders start saying he is a better person than his highly educated cousin who did not even attend the last funeral rites of their aunt just because he was attending studies abroad. But then the wife is grumbling at his extravagance at her expense, and he uses the proceeds from the eighth tonne to buy her new dresses, perfumes and shoes.

With only two tonnes left, our trader gets serious. No more spending because all the money is needed for restocking. He sells the remaining cement, and is told by the manufacturer that he can buy a minimum of ten tonnes at factory price. Because he has to satisfy his customers, he stocks two tonnes from a nearby fellow trader, which he sells at no profit. That is when another trader advises him to join hands so they can buy ten tonnes at the manufacturer's price between several of them. They collect the money and entrust it to one of their number, who reports it lost the next day.

He gives them an unconvincing tale of the lorry which he had hired but did not know that it had no licence and had been impounded by the revenue police, along with their cement. He says he is only lucky not to have been arrested with the driver. They are not convinced but they cannot do anything about it. It is time for our young trader to surrender the shop to a more serious trader, and return to being a broker for other shopkeepers. He spends most of the commissions he gets on witch doctors to tell him who was behind his downfall from a prosperous cement dealer to a miserable broker.

The big-time businessman has more staying power, and therefore does more damage. He has connections, a big name and doesn't go down so easily. He has probably lived abroad for a few months and when he gets a business idea, he makes sure a few high-ranking people learn about it. Finally, he gets one of the big names in politics to join him as a silent partner, for purposes of kicking slow bureaucrats and bankers into action.

The projects kick off well, with some press coverage about how it is going to earn the country lots of badly needed foreign exchange and employ so many people. The government minister who launches it calls upon the rest of the Ugandan business community to emulate our man's example, to create jobs and bring in skills gathered from overseas, and so on.

After a few months, our man starts getting more orders from abroad than he can supply. He has to expand his working capital, and fast. He goes to his bankers who are well aware of the viability of his project. They give him an overdraft of $100,000. He has never seen such a figure on his account, any account for that matter. These are monies you read about in newspapers regarding government projects! To have it at his command! Unbelievable. Now that he is expanding, he needs manpower. An uncle's son who has had no job since he left college is brought in as storekeeper. His wife's younger sister becomes front-office manager while his sister's wayward son is employed as executive driver.

All the dreams he has had since childhood come vividly to his head and lock out common sense that the bank's money was intended for buying raw materials. He orders the latest four-wheel drive car – bigger than his neighbour's – and a smaller but equally chic one for his wife. When his glittering new machine gets a dent at his narrow gate as his inexperienced teenage son tries to manoeuvre it, he decides to quit the bad neighbourhood.

Encouraged by his wife who says the jealous neighbours were about to plot for robbers to attack them, they move house to Kololo hill where the next-door neighbour is an ambassador and the surroundings are more conducive to raising children because the stiff rent keeps out ordinary families. With about ten thousand dollars left on the overdraft account, our man orders some raw materials.

As he starts processing the big orders, the bank asks for its first repayment instalment. This he manages somehow, remaining with no cash. Workers' salaries start delaying. The second overdraft instalment falls due and there isn't enough money to pay. After many negotiations, the bank quietly takes over collections. They find a new businessman to purchase the factory. After all creditors are paid, our man is paid the remaining few thousand dollars, which he uses to join politics.

Politician

History has been very unkind to Ugandan politicians. While their counterparts in neighbouring Kenya were waging the bitter Mau Mau war to dismantle a vicious colonial machinery, history was busy conspiring to grant Uganda independence without a single shot being fired. While other Africans were agitating to recover their land, which had been occupied by the colonial settlers, the British were helping Ugandans consolidate their traditional systems that guaranteed ownership and access to land. This denied the elite a platform on which to agitate.

Although Winston Churchill was so taken up by the natural beauty of the country that he summarised his entire African journey in three words, 'Concentrate on Uganda', his countrymen never settled here in large numbers and preferred to leave the traditional administrative structures largely unaltered. They ruled the country indirectly, flatteringly assuring us that it was not a colony, but a protectorate. With fertile soils and a conducive climate at the disposal of the naturally capitalistic local society, there was no need to whip the natives into working; being integrated into the world market system was all they wanted and the profit motive took care of the rest. Her majesty's government built infrastructure and then sat back to collect revenue from the three C's - Cotton, Coffee and Copper.

9

Britain even borrowed a few thousand pounds from Uganda, which were still unpaid at the close of the 20th century.

When the struggles for independence were sweeping across Africa, our forefathers joined in, as a fashion, demanding self-rule. To be fair to them, they had some bitter grievances, like the right to drink European brands of beer, which they had been denied until after the Second World War. So the British conceded and allowed Ugandan Africans to drink European beer, and local industries to bottle it were set up.

British and French missionaries had built nice schools across the country that gave an elitist education to children who were described as the leaders of tomorrow. Some lucky Kenyans and Tanzanians who managed to make it to the Ugandan schools, and the famous Makerere University College, were poised to take up leadership positions in their countries at the dawn of independence. Their Ugandan contemporaries also intensified their demand for independence. The British called them over for a meeting in England, where they amicably worked out the handover of the famous instruments of power. So on October 9, 1962, we got our nice black-yellow-red striped flag, played our beautiful three-stanza national anthem and the few colonial managers went home, vacating their nice offices and residences to the new leaders.

With no scars to show for their independence 'struggle', the Ugandan leaders continued to party.

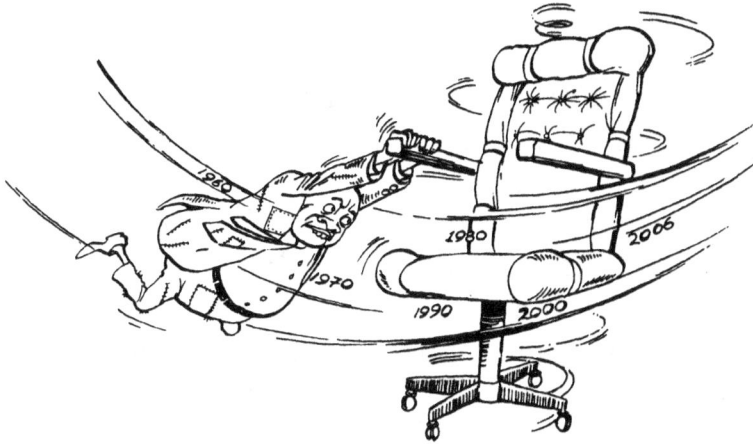

Some politicians soon got bored with the party and tried to engage the new rulers in frank debate, the way they had done with the British. They soon discovered, from behind locked prison doors, that the new leaders did not entertain debate. Criticism was regarded as subversion and, before 1970, opposition became equal to treason, officially. Politicians soon learnt that if you had anything to say, you either left the country or kept quiet. They then developed the new art of talking politics.

Even long after the departure of the profoundly corrupt and dictatorial regimes of the seventies, politicians haven't changed much. Even physically, some individuals have remained on the scene for 40 years as top national leaders. Men who were senior cabinet ministers at independence in 1962 were still around in 2002, lobbying for political jobs from a president who was hardly a teenager when they were in charge of the country 40 years earlier.

Unlike other professions, a politician's job in Uganda doesn't require much upgrading with changing technologies. You just need to say the same things at all occasions: Castigate the past regimes, then call upon the masses to redouble their efforts and to rally behind the able and wise leadership of the current president. An ageing Briton who left the country in 1962 after hearing a political speech and returned in 2002 was puzzled on listening to a member of parliament speak. It was as if he had never left the country for even a week.

While making a political speech, try as much as possible to sound like the president. If he has a high-pitched voice, make yours even higher. If he pauses to adjust his glasses, do the same. Start by acquiring a pair of plain ones if you have no eye defect. Try and adopt his hairstyle. If he parts his hair, do the same to yours. If he is bald-headed, for heaven's sake get clean-shaven immediately. If he speaks with a slight stammer when he is agitated, stammer as well. But don't overdo it. The idea is for people to confuse your voice and his. So, when the masses are listening on radio, or at a big rally where most cannot see who has the microphone in the sheltered VIP platform, they ask whether it is you or the president speaking.

The other important thing, if you are to survive long in the lucrative office, is to give the impression that you are close to the big man. That way, your rivals will hesitate to do anything to undermine you. Whenever you are getting out of your office, instruct the secretary to tell all callers that you have gone to State House. Whenever you miss an appointment, apologise profusely later, explaining that you had been summoned at short notice to the big man's home. If it has been reported in the news that the president is camping in Gulu, say you had been urgently called to Gulu.

Punctuate all your speeches with references to conversations with the president. Don't quote meetings that were attended by other people. No. Just say, "The other day I was telling the president about this problem and he also agreed that..." Lines picked like this from a five-minute meeting you had with the man two years ago can serve you well on different occasions. You don't have to worry that anybody is keeping track of it. Remember to express your awe of the man as someone close would, say how it is hard to keep pace with him, how he is so tireless and how marathon meetings with him require you to be alert all the time.

If, in your enthusiasm to impress people with your power, you ever make a silly statement that you regret, do what everybody else does – blame the press. "I was misquoted" is the politician's defence worldwide, why bother to invent anything new?

When you suspect that a reshuffle is about to take place, make drastic statements about how right the president always is. Describe him using terms usually reserved for God. Castigate the opposition ruthlessly. Warn any region that fails to support the president that they will be marginalised in the allocation of development resources.

Should the president be so unkind as to still drop you in the reshuffle, seek private audience with him to express your innocence and unwavering support for him. If his aides make it difficult for you to see him, try and locate the sister of a senior minister's second wife and implore her to tell her sister to tell her husband to tell the president at the earliest opportunity that some people are blocking you from delivering a sensitive piece of information that is vital to his current pet project.

Never waste the chance once you finally get to see him. You can kneel down, cry, and threaten to commit suicide, anything. After all, it is in private. He will be the only one seeing you, and he has seen worse things than that. Appeal to his parental heart and tell him your children are still going to school, and implore him to give them a chance to complete their education – by giving you a job.

If there are no places in cabinet, tell him to make you a junior minister at least. If those slots are also filled up, remind him that you can be a good presidential advisor, whatever that means. What matters is that there is always room for another presidential advisor, and he doesn't need to ask for your advice. But things might be tough and the man doesn't want to appoint you as an advisor. Don't lose heart. Ask him to make you an ambassador to one of the smaller countries. Don't set your target too high. If this fails, you can settle for Resident District Commissioner (RDC). Remind him that you had just started constructing your house and if it remains unfinished, this will reflect badly on his government, showing that leaders cannot set a good example.

It is after such efforts to see the president fail that you set plan B in motion – to become a critic. This becomes especially urgent when you lose that long-running tender to deliver supplies to a government department through third parties, and the banks start calling in your overdrafts. When the kiosk operator near your house starts demanding cash up-front for all the groceries, you have nothing to lose anymore and you can now use bare knuckles.

If you want to be a successful critic, do not speak a lot. You wait for the right moment like one of the many seminars in town, and then strike like lightning. Just make a short remark about the 'massive corruption' that has compounded the problem being discussed. When you are contacted by the reporters later to elaborate, you describe how unnamed powerful persons blocked your efforts to streamline things. Come up with a wildly huge figure of monies lost because your advice was overruled. Then you keep quiet for a week. If there is no message from high up, you leak more damaging information about your rival and then 'accidentally' turn up at another seminar where you drop another bombshell. This is the right time to add that sometimes people are justified to go to the bush and rebel against the government. If security people call you to ask you a few questions after this, you become a celebrity, a martyr. Soon you will become a darling of the press. Until you get rehabilitated by being called back into government.

The change you undergo is physically visible in the form of the chauffeured newest car in vogue with senior officials, bodyguards and a new, confident pose. It is then time for your rivals to hide their heads, lie low for a while as you spit fire about 'disgruntled elements', 'wolves in sheep skin', 'agents of foreign interests' and some local terms like 'night dancers'. Whenever it comes, enjoy your day in the sun, because you never know when your fortunes will next take a nose-dive, as the political cycle continues to turn.

Foreign Investor

Do you want to become rich? Just read the three-word conclusion Winston Churchill wrote at the end of his book *My Africa Journey*: "Concentrate on Uganda". All you need is spend a year or two enjoying the sunshine, speaking a lot of finance jargon and adopting an aristocratic pose as you accept the maximum respect accorded to you by the local officials. This is what you get as a 'foreign investor', a title only surpassed by that of 'President of the Republic' in carrying weight in Kampala.

To join that revered class, and become a millionaire in the process as well, is an easy process – but you have to be a foreigner and remain one. It helps if you come from Europe, America or Asia. It won't be easy at all if you come from Africa; we have enough Africans around. The only exception is of course South Africa and northern Africa. If you are from the other parts where Africans are black, you will have to work hard to become rich here, which you may as well do in your own country without coming to eat matoke (cooked bananas)and nsenene (seasonal green grasshoppers) and pretending that you like their taste like us.

But if you belong to the earlier categories, this is how to become a financial prince. First you read those free IMF/World Bank newsletters and identify a new line of credit being extended to Uganda. It could be for something like a livestock local feeds development programme, a promotion of fresh-water fish exports programme, or a programme for the harnessing of wind energy to supplement hydro-electric power in sub-Saharan Africa. Don't be scared by the long, strange names. In fact the more weird it sounds the more lucrative and less likely to have competition.

What you do after identifying the sector is to set up a company with an equally strange-sounding name. Pay the equivalent of $50 to a struggling, downmarket lawyer and you will have the company incorporated and duly registered in Uganda. After you get your papers, sever all links with the small-time lawyer because you just used him to save money. Associating with him could become a liability in circles that matter. This is because Ugandan society is arranged in circles, and he belongs to a circle that does not matter.

From here you go alone to the Uganda Investment Authority offices. You will find the UIA fellows very hungry for foreign investors and they will hug you breathless. Demand to speak to the highest-ranking person available. As they fall all over themselves to please you, maintain an air of aloofness as you describe the project that you want to set up. Use the name of the president, but sparingly. Just say when he visited your country you mentioned the project to him and he directed you to the UIA. Just mention his name once again before departure, saying you are pleased the officials have been as

helpful as he said they would. Then say you will mention it to him when you meet him on the ...er... check your diary and pick a date three weeks ahead, when your company president will be in Kampala to check on the progress of the paperwork.

These little games are necessary to beat the bureaucracy. Remember a big investor like you does not have much time to deal with clerks. So the officers should be made to know that you are in touch with the high offices. That way, they will breathe down the necks of all the smaller fellows who process licences and permits.

You need to meet the right people as you move towards the implementation stage. There are about three circles of influential people in Kampala. You will never reach the innermost circle, you just need to sound like you can. But the second ring consists of a few senior ministers – not all – and a few top security men. There are also some big business people in the second ring, a few top lawyers and a few non-political top public officials like heads of statutory bodies. The people in this second ring of power have one thing in common – direct access to the people in the innermost ring – the centre.

Your immediate target is to get accepted in the second ring. Lift a phone and call one of them. Don't make your native accent any easier. The newer in Kampala you sound the better. Go to the guy's office and introduce your project. Invite him back to your hotel. He may come or suggest that you meet at the club or one of the top hotels in the city. Once there, you will be surprised how small a country it is. A few evenings there and you will know most of the members of the second ring – the ring that matters. It is then time to sell your project – all the time sounding like it is at an advanced stage.

Once the other UIA chaps have secured all the licences for you, return to your country and locate the oldest machinery in the junkyards that is about to be boarded off. Help the owners with the disposal and ship it off towards Uganda. Set up a briefcase company in your own country so it becomes the supplier of the 'modern' equipment. This 'company' should invoice your Ugandan company in the millions of dollars. Back in Uganda, lease a plot of land and start constructing some factory-like premises.

Now your friends from the second ring have to prove their worth. You submit your application for a loan from the other line of credit, and your friends have to ensure government gives it the strongest backing. Finally the money is released – to the foreign supplier who is yourself. The old equipment arrives in the country and you install it. Using about ten percent of the entire loan, which is safely in your account back home, you complete the modest factory building, install the old machines and order some raw materials.

You launch the factory with a lot of noise, getting the highest-ranking official possible to commission the plant. Powerful speeches are made about the foreign exchange your company will save the country, the hundreds of Ugandans you will employ when you operate at full capacity and the many backward and forward linkages that will be created.

Don't forget to offer shareholding and directorships to your Ugandan friends from the second ring. Ugandans in the third ring of influence, who number in their hundreds and include members of parliament and civil servants, will flood the people in the second ring with requests for jobs for their relatives. Suddenly, everyone will be talking nicely about your company. Paint its very bright logo on a couple of secondhand vans and sponsor an old soap opera on the national television. It is quite cheap but will do wonders for your image. Pay very good wages, by local standards; you need some genuine tears when the company goes bust.

If the junk machinery performs for several months, well and good. You can even start paying off some of the loan. If it breaks down, order some spares which probably do not exist anymore. By now you should have identified the culprits to blame for not prospering fast enough. High electricity and water tariffs, corrupt government officials, bad weather, crop failure, slow disbursement of credit funds for this and that component or customs officials who delayed your perishable input. Make alot of noise and get your friends in the second ring to tell their other friends about it. Before you know it, the entire public will be blaming somebody for your problems. If any local technician asks you about the junk machines, explain to him with a lot of anger about the vital spares that the customs people have denied you authorisation to import. Technicians don't know these things. He will grow to hate the customs people with a passion, for rendering him jobless. He will tell his family how they are suffering because his foreign boss refused to bribe the customs officials.

Around this time, you should make some urgent trips abroad to try and sort out things. Depending on how irredeemable your project is, you will decide whether to file for bankruptcy while abroad or return personally to do it Kampala. Also, depending on how deeply you fall in love with this bewitching land of ours, you can even stay on and start another project. When it fails, you will become

22

yet richer in the process. Never mind about the unpaid loans. The receivers will try to make the company work and when it finally collapses, it will have died in somebody else's hands. Nobody will bother you and the debt will join the mountain several billions of dollars the country owes. Don't waste time thinking of the debt burden for the wretched Ugandans. The future generations will pay. It is their problem, not yours.

Civil Servant

I am the Ugandan civil servant; duly enrolled by the Public Service Commission. I am therefore a permanent and pensionable officer. For many years I read the civil service Standing Orders, Rules and Regulations and the Code of Conduct. I used to believe in them. That was until the World Bank and International Monetary Fund conspired with the Government of Uganda to bring Structural Adjustment Programmes, appropriately called SAPs, to sap all my morale. Under the Public Service Review and Restructuring Programme, they introduced a dangerous animal called retrenchment. Many of my old friends and a few of my enemies got retrenched. After the massive retrenchment exercise, they even proposed that civil servants be employed on short contracts. Yet we went to school and worked hard in order to become permanent and pensionable! Now they are changing the rules mid-course. Such injustice! I now no longer refer to all the pamphlets they gave me when I joined the civil service. I now follow the Bible. Not all of it: I only need Ecclesiastes Chapter Three. It sums up all my philosophy, which has helped me survive since the terrible SAPs were introduced.

ECCLESIASTES CHAPTER 3:
In the civil service, there is a time for everything;
A time to be hired and a time to be fired;
A time to be paid and a time to be taxed;
A time for promotion and a time for demotion;
A time to work and a time to avoid work;
A time be early and a time to be late;
A day to be present and a day to be absent;
A time to tell the truth and a time to lie;
A time to laugh and a time to cry;
A time to assist colleagues and a time to undermine them;
A time to promote government plans and a time to
sabotage them.

Ever since I started following this part of the
Bible, I have found peace of mind and everything
is running smoothly. I know I am one of the highly
endangered species, what with retrenchment, and
I find fortitude in the Bible. Every day I recite the
above verses and live according to them.

I have discovered how to preserve my skin in all turbulent situations because if I am sacked I will not be able to serve my country. Remember our national motto says 'For God and my Country'. So to remain in service, if my boss says 'Jump!' I only ask, 'How high?' and when he says 'Bend!' mine is to ask how low. And should I get a chance to talk to his boss, I don't waste the opportunity; I tell them all his mistakes without appearing to report him.

I have also over time designed several survival strategies. The guiding principle is to ensure that I use minimum effort and get maximum benefits. I believe that in all disciplines, fields and sectors, that is the measure of efficiency – maximising output while using minimum input. So the fewer days I work to complete the month, the more I consider myself efficient. I see absolutely no reason to report for five days a week for work which I can do in two or three days. So I ensure that I report to the office on those days when the boss needs to hold a meeting with me; days when my signature is required on documents - especially when the owners of the documents need to thank me in tangible terms and on days when my accumulated claims have to be paid by the cash office.

Of course on the days I do not report to office I am working very hard. Even my mileage and hotel accommodation claims indicate so. I have become so efficient that I can be in several places at a go. So when I am in the field on days when I am not working at the office, the jacket on the backrest of my chair indicates that I am around.

My colleagues and I have developed a vocabulary that is very useful and my secretary has mastered it. So when you call the office and I am not at my desk, she will select the appropriate term:

"He is within" – By this she means that I am somewhere in the building, so don't think that I have dodged work or have gone to town to do other things.

"He just stepped out" – This she says when I left the office several hours ago, and when I return I will return your call, claiming that when you called I had just stepped out, probably to an office next door.

"He is around" – This means almost the same as the above, but used only with people of lower rank than mine, while 'just stepped out' is for people who can determine my fate.

"He is in the field" – This is what she says when I have not reported for duty at all and do not intend to at all that day.

I do not do all this, or fail to do so much, because of being a bad person. It is the government that taught me its ways. Ever since inflation set in way back in the mid-seventies and civil service wages were not adjusted accordingly, government pretends to pay its workers and we also pretend to work for it. They have always promised us a living wage but it only remains that – a promise. In reality, they only pay me enough money to sustain me with my family for five days in return for a whole month's work. So when government pretends that my salary is enough, I also pretend to do enough work. That way, we have struck a harmonious compromise. We pretend to be good to each other and life continues. Or so it will, until the day they will tell me that my services are no longer required. That is when they will give me my retirement package worth several thousand dollars, which I will use to join politics.

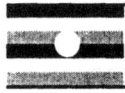

▰▰◑▰ Doctor

Before the days of gun rule, all was simply rosy for us doctors. A medical doctor was revered more than the bishop. The status society accorded us was simply out of this world. Of course the public never got an inkling of what we did. First of all, they thought we were all surgeons. So when a young lady finished medical school, on her graduation day lengthy speeches would be made about how she can open up anybody's brain and put it back in place, after healing it of course. Doctors were thus feared. It took a doctor to marry another doctor. No ordinary being could dare entertain thoughts of getting that close to us. Our coats were holier than a bishop's robes.

Then came the military government in the early seventies. The military rulers had a special penchant for our blood. They killed our colleagues by the dozen, for no reason other than being a doctor. That must have been the time the ordinary people started realising that we were also human. They saw us fleeing for dear life, as the soldier boys came for our necks. To this day, we have never worked out why they hated us so much. What we know is that they forced us to think of personal survival first all the time. Previously, doctors were well paid, well housed and concentrated all their time on treating patients and carrying out research. Then came the insecurity and the accompanying triple-digit inflation that made a doctor's salary meaningless. You could import neither drugs nor equipment. Most doctors fled to Southern Africa and Europe. Those who stayed kept a low profile and learnt how to survive. That is when the medics became part and parcel of the Ugandan society and had to learn fast the ways of the street. Long after the military boys have gone, the doctors still operate by the survival instinct.

First, we had to invent the 'dual band' system. This is a method of work whereby you keep one leg in government and another in a private clinic. We had never been entrepreneurs but the circumstances made all of us open private clinics. Our clinics and the government hospitals feed each other in a symbiotic relationship. When we get a patient at the public hospital, we prescribe for them the drug that they need. Because that drug is not available at the (free) government hospital, we refer the patient to our clinic, where they can buy the drug. If we didn't direct them to where the drug could be found they would die, wouldn't they?

Similarly, our private patients who come only to the clinic may sometimes need an operation before a sophisticated examination and the facilities for this are at the government hospital. You see, our clinics are just small consultation rooms and boxes of drugs – and our brains. So we admit our private patients to the government facilities for surgery and complicated treatment. That is why you must remain in the big public hospital where you make

an appearance on known days and hours every week, and also be in the private practice where the patients who pay come.

Sometimes the private clinic can be very busy because of your seniority and fame. That is when you recruit younger doctors from the government hospital to come and see the bulk of the patients. But some patients insist on being seen only by the senior doctor – I told you how aristocratic Ugandans can be, especially when they get money. An illiterate trader will insist a junior doctor cannot treat him. A politician will consult only with the owner of the clinic. So the only way to ease such congestion of arrogant patients is to charge them stiffly for consultation, but they still pay. Then they go and boast, telling their friends how much they paid you to treat them.

Another nice 'problem' comes when you successfully treat an influential person or a member of his family. That is when you start getting appointments you had never dreamed of and additional responsibilities that reduce the time you used to have for attending to patients. You find yourself a consultant on this and that programme. Then the influential persons start pressing you to stand for parliament, assuring you of all the support. You find yourself attending meeting after meeting of a non-medical nature and eventually, as has happened to many of our colleagues, you end up a minister in government. Yet with all these, you somehow find time to attend to some of your patients.

At the turn of the millennium, we started getting younger doctors coming back from overseas with all sorts of computer diagnostic gadgetry. They have helped ease the congestion at our clinics as many patients flock to them. Others have opened modern private hospitals where patients are pampered as if they are in the business class of a modern airliner. But the older generation who appreciate the human element more than the blips of the digital equipment have stuck with us. All in all, we are all making lots of money and these days we can stand in the community of upright, dignified men and get respected as of old.

Driver

A famous American journalist and author, David Lamb, said in his book *The Africans* that the only time an African is in a hurry is when he is behind a wheel. The Ugandan is no exception. Little wonder then that in spite of having the lowest vehicle per capita ratio in the world, our continent also lays claim to a fatal accident rate that is ten times higher than that of London and New York. Sensible car driving has simply refused to blend with our culture.

The Ugandan driver starts his career by buying a driving licence. He then starts looking for someone to teach him how to drive.

There are three types of drivers – the taxi drivers, the private car driver called 'my car' and the institutional driver. By 'taxi', in Uganda we mean a minibus commuter which carries 14 passengers but the number can increase if there is no traffic policeman in sight. If you want a taxi, as in a cab, you have to ask for a 'special'. You see, we have also made our contribution to the growth of the English language.

Back to the training of the drivers. After buying the driver's licence, you look for a driving instructor. That is when you are told that before learning to drive, you need a provisional driving permit, otherwise you can be arrested along with your instructor. So you apply for and instantly get the provisional licence, valid for 90 days.

Your choice of instructor depends on what car you intend to drive. If you are a housewife or young lady who has just bought a car, you are better off going to YWCA where they have women instructors. In the other so-called driving schools, the young male instructors want to help your leg press down the clutch, with their hand.

All the time while learning, remember to hide your driving permit – which shows you are a qualified driver. Don't even tell your instructor that you are already a financially qualified driver. The instructor will take you through the quiet roads of the upmarket suburb of Kololo, and on Sundays take you downtown when the traffic is low. After two or three weeks, he will start preparing you for the test. You can bolt then, and stop the training. Then you start driving your own car, learning the road signs slowly. While going to work, you have to start extremely early, when there are very few cars on the road, and return very late when the traffic has eased. This also helps you gain experience in night driving.

If your intention is to drive a 'taxi', you don't need an instructor. You buy the licence and start driving. If you are lucky, you may not kill yourself and the passengers before you perfect the skills.

If your intention is to get a job as a driver in a company or government department, the key thing is to get the job after buying the licence. Then pay someone with a vehicle of relevant weight to take you through a crash programme so that by the time

you report for duty, you can whistle confidently as you reverse into your new boss's compound to pick him up in the morning. Take care not to run over his kids.

Once on the road, what matters most is confidence. Learn to sneer at other drivers and in a traffic jam, ask the fellow disputing the lane with you if he just bought his license, unlike you who passed the driving test. When you approach a junction, never leave any empty space in front of you. Whether you can clear the junction or not, enter it anyway. A thick jam will build up on your side. Regard it and nod with satisfaction. Then look

35

behind you in the rearview mirror and behold the nice, long, snakelike jam growing longer by the second. Savour this all, take a deep breath and smile. Roll up your windows to close out the impatient hooting as the fellows you have blocked build up blood pressure like yours.

Like the British, we keep left while driving. But that is only while driving on a straight stretch. At junctions, left and right stop making sense - just take the shortest straight line to your objective. Jam on the brakes when you are almost head-on with the fellow from the opposite direction who insists on keeping left. What are brakes for, anyway?

Should your bumper be slightly tapped by another car, stop right there and then and block all the other vehicles. Jump out of yours, work up a temper fit to light a match and ask the other driver what is wrong with his head. Throw the keys at him and tell him you need your car the next day in perfect condition. Do not accept to drive away until the other motorist has paid you enough money to fill your tank at the next filling station. That is what you needed the money for anyway because the slight scratch on your bumper can remain unnoticed until you sell off the car next year.

Warning to foreigners: Whenever you see a truck coming from ahead, especially from the direction of Kenya, get off the road completely. While most drivers keep left, truck drivers keep the middle. They never look to see who else is on the road. They are too busy chewing certain leaves to see you. The leaves keep them awake, they claim.

PS: Although in Uganda it is against the law to drink and drive, hardly anybody has ever been prosecuted for this dangerous crime. It would appear, therefore, that you can drive while drinking beer – it is actually prestigious to be seen holding the steering wheel with one hand while the other is holding a bottle of beer to your mouth. Unlike other countries where you get arrested for drink driving, talking on a mobile phone while driving or failing to fasten your seat belt while in the front seat, in Uganda it is perfectly normal to drive after drinking heavily. Many old men are lifted up after passing out on bar floors and placed behind the wheel. They then drive home where they pass out at the gate. After that the big son comes and parks the car.

But some people drive without drinking alcohol. Social researchers might one day find out why some Ugandan drivers don't drink.

◖ Emigrant: Kyeyo

Half of the Ugandans would rather be out of Uganda, doing menial jobs called *kyeyo*. The word *kyeyo* means a large broom, symbolising the unskilled jobs in Europe and North America which are believed to pay ten times more than a professional's salary in Kampala.

Photos sent by relatives of friends who made it to Europe and North America have done a lot to convince our people that a British or US visa is the key to paradise. And so most young people's dream is to get a chance to go for *kyeyo* abroad. You can't convince a Ugandan youth that life out there can be tough. So don't even try.

The long process to get the coveted visa takes on average about three years and starts as soon as the aspiring emigrant leaves college. Incited by the photos he kept seeing for three years in his room-mate's album of a young man standing in snow, wearing thick clothes complete with gloves and head covering, our young man applies for a passport. This he gets in a couple of weeks since the process was made easier towards the end of the twentieth century. There is a minor celebration with close friends over the acquisition of the vital document.

Working closely with an emigration 'consultant' who could be an airline worker or a self-styled travel agent, the young man embarks on the second phase

of leaving Uganda. He secures a letter of invitation from people living abroad. He may know the person inviting him, provided this person has enough bank balance in his account. If he knows nobody abroad, the 'consultant' provides one – for a fee. Armed with the letter, he proceeds to the embassy and asks for a visa application form. While filling this, what he indicates as the objective of the visit depends on the season. The consultants know what works best at a given time. It could be attending to a sick relative, attending a brother's wedding, taking part in a seminar or even a short holiday. School delegations travelling for sports or cultural programmes can be made to include aspiring emigrants, who sometimes have to revise their age downwards, and a different passport acquired for the purpose. One time there were three hundred visa applications for a ten-man band that was going to play in the States when the Kabaka (Buganda's cultural king) was visiting the Ugandan community in North America. All the women applicants said they were dancers, while the men claimed to play some instrument that has no name in English.

The most difficult part is the visa interview at the embassy. The US interviews are said to be the toughest, especially after the 2001 September 11 terrorist attacks. The UK interviews are not so tough but then everyone wants to go there and the queues at the British High Commission are ridiculously long, with applicants at times starting to line up before midnight for an interview for eight o'clock the next morning. In those queues, there are people who are trying for the visa for the fourth or fifth time, and they keep giving tips on how to answer the questions to first-timers. Sometimes when an application is rejected, one has to secure a new identity and a new passport to try again.

The preparation for the interview is a thorough, secret exercise. The 'consultant' takes the applicant through a serious rehearsal in a dingy downtown office, and will not let him go for the interview until he has mastered all his lines. The applicant, who may be as broke as a church mouse, is equipped with a bank statement that shows he has millions of shillings in savings, and can confidently explain how he accumulated them. To prove further that he has an economic stake in Uganda, which he wouldn't abandon for a menial job abroad, he also has copies of land titles.

Still many people fail the interview, and have to keep trying, sometimes changing identity. If our young man is lucky and gets the precious visa, he starts the process of hunting for money to match a fraction of his claimed worth. Secondhand cars, small slum houses and parents' land have been sold to purchase air tickets and raise pocket money for the *kyeyo* people.

A sad observation about independent Africa is that while our grandparents were forcefully dragged from Africa, packed in ship holds for the often-fatal journey to go and work in America, today their grandchildren will go to all lengths including borrowing and telling lies to take themselves there.

The lies do not end after boarding the British Airways flight at Entebbe airport. Once on board, the *kyeyo* boy has to switch mental gears, and start practising the different story he will tell about himself once he lands in the 'promised land'. Before his three-month visa expires, he must have lodged his application for political asylum. And to do this he must be prepared to swear convincingly how his life was in grave danger because he was a human rights activist at the university. He should be able to recount harrowing experiences of torture in security cells and manifest trauma symptoms as he recalls how the torture sergeant's instruments worked on his body.

Eventually our young man settles in, doing three or four jobs around the clock in order to buy that coveted BMW and move out of the apartment he has been sharing with several other Ugandans. Remembering his vows to become rich in five years, he starts sending his savings to his brother back home to buy a town plot and construct a semi-detached mansion for himself. He estimates that this will generate income for him on completion, turning him into a proud investor. The process goes on for a couple of years, with the brother sending him progress photographs of the house under construction. These he proudly shows to fellow immigrant workers, and they drink to his growing investment portfolio.

After finally acquiring permanent residence in his host country, he can now return to Uganda, the political persecution story forgotten, to check on his investments. That is when the brother who was in charge of construction disappears. Several weeks of searching for the mansion yields nothing, and the dejected *kyeyo* man returns 'home' abroad, swearing not to trust his relatives again.

But once there, boredom and loneliness soon overcome him and he sends a message asking his relatives to find a suitable girl for him to marry. The search party, armed with pictures of the young man leaning against his BMW, has a very easy job. About five girls are short-listed and when he comes to Kampala, he makes his pick. After the relevant medical tests, a hasty wedding is arranged and the couple returns.

A few of these marriages have worked. Most have ended in separation as the girls, after getting their own resident status, start quietly looking for their separate opportunities in different towns with the help of older Ugandan women who went there earlier. After a couple of years as a professional wife, she surprises her husband by moving out. That is when our immigrant brother finally matures into an accomplished, permanent *kyeyo* man. He makes the appropriate vows never to trust Ugandans again in his life, cuts off links with family and former friends and prepares for retirement abroad. No wonder, only about one in a thousand Ugandans who go abroad to make money 'just for five years' ever comes back.

Rumours

Like the ancient city of Rome, Kampala too was built on seven hills – originally. By 1980 all the formal channels of information like the media broke down or were no longer reliable. The rumour machine took over to 'inform' the public during those years of unstable government. Several times a day, rumours would fly around about the government being overthrown, the president going into hiding or senior army officers staging a mutiny. That is how the humorous president Godfrey Binaisa came to describe Kampala as the city of seven rumours a day. The implication was that seven rumours descended into the city every day, one from each hill.

But with the rapid growth towards the close of the last century, the city started engulfing more hills. By the fortieth independence anniversary, Kampala sat firmly on 21 hills. And with the coming of mobile phones and FM radio stations, the speed at which the rumours travel and multiply increased many times over. The traditional transportation of rumours by rickety taxis and overloaded buses became obsolete as higher technology took over. With so many private radio stations on air and a mobile phone in every other person's hand, Kampala entered the information age with an unassailable claim to the title of Rumoursville.

The city rumour machine was invented during

the last years of colonial rule. Political rumours were churned out of what was then called Radio Katwe. Katwe is a Kampala slum that was never invaded by Asian traders or European offices. It remained a purely African neighbourhood, also renowned for crude technological innovations. When you are passing on a political rumour and you are asked for your source of information, you answer that you heard it on Radio Katwe. That way, you are absolved of responsibility should the rumour turn out to be false.

Ugandans create rumours just about anything. However, their favourite topics are politics, money, sex and death. Political rumours are mostly about reshuffles and appointments. Once a rumour hits the streets that there is a cabinet reshuffle in the making, it grows to include who is about to get appointed and who is facing the sack.

That is when the circus starts. When people who have been shouting a lot of praises for the president get told that they will soon be ministers, their conduct changes immediately. They start writing their inaugural speeches, get fitted for new suits, start patronising more respectable clubs and generally carry themselves with a more confident gait. In the anticipation that ensues, they get new friends, those who have been distant acquaintances suddenly become closer and the aspirants start getting too many unnecessary smiles and handshakes. The salesmen don't lose time and start making them offers of cars and houses. It is only in a few cases that a rumoured appointment actually takes place. But still people continue believing rumours about impending appointments and go to unnecessary expenses to prepare for the new status that never materialises.

When we are not gossiping about imaginary appointments, we sometimes tackle the morbid subject of death. When a prominent person dies in Kampala, a few days later you should expect news of the death of another prominent person. By coincidence, prominent people sometimes die in twos or threes, though their deaths are unrelated. So when one prominent person dies, news follows of another one who has died. Then you have to wait to know for sure whether he has really died, or it is just the rumour machine working overtime.

Sometimes false rumours of death just emerge out of the blue. It seems we are always waiting for someone to die. It may be an exiled politician who is pronounced dead by the rumour machine; it may be a relative of a minister or it could even be a new-born baby of an opposition politician. There is simply no formula. It is all about creativity.

The rumour starts from a very bored person who decides that a certain minister is dead. Mr Rumour Manufacturer picks up his cellular phone, goes through the directory and selects the number for his friend, Mr Loud Mouth, whom he calls and asks, "Have you heard that Honourable Smart is dead?" Loud Mouth says he is not yet aware. Immediately the conversation ends, Loud Mouth in turn calls another person, not asking, but telling him that Hon. Smart is dead. He says he got it from an inside source.

The third person then calls his wife. He does not want to sound that he has second hand information. He says his very close friend in government has just told him that Hon. Smart is dead, but she should not tell the neighbours or her friends because they have not yet announced it officially. That ensures that the neighbours will be told immediately. She tells the news, saying that he died abroad while on a secret mission, and the government is trying to smuggle the body back before announcing the man's death.

There is a sense of importance in appearing to know important news first. The next one hour registers unusually heavy traffic on the mobile phone networks, as everyone is trying to pass on the news. Within an hour of the initial generation of the rumour, everyone in Kampala has heard the news. Hon. Smart's house phone is ringing off the hook. His wife is a bit hysterical, though she has already spoken with him at his upcountry hotel where he went to carry out some state duties.

Hon. Smart's assistant finally rings the local radio station to refute the rumour. That adds fuel to the fire. People who have already got the rumour just hear his name and the word death on radio and conclude the man is dead. "He is dead," different callers say. "It is even on the radio."

Then someone calls Mrs Smart and assures her that the radio is announcing her husband's death. A furious Mrs Smart calls the radio station, threatening to sue them and have their broadcasting licence revoked. She calls another radio station to refute the malicious allegations that her husband is dead. The second station gleefully refutes the 'baseless rumour' being peddled by 'sections of the media' that Hon. Smart is dead. They even ring Smart and put his voice on air as he refutes the rumour. So the radio station that first refuted the story is blamed for the 'malicious rumour'. Now that a culprit is found, the story can end there. The only troublesome rumours are those where there is nobody to blame. The rumours about sex do not ignite the city like the death ones do. But they keep conversations going for long hours in cafes, bars and of course, offices. Remember offices are places where people gossip and sometimes do some work.

Kampala is a small city where everybody knows every rich person and every beautiful woman. So there is always someone weaving a connection between one person and another. Of course the rumour is much better when both are married to different persons. It is a town where everybody can speak authoritatively about the sex lives of political and religious leaders. Everybody speaks confidently about which minister's wife has eloped with the driver and which rally driver has made a schoolgirl pregnant. People simply love sex talk.

When the rumour machine is not killing dignitaries or joining them in bed, it does some work on their fortunes. That is when you will hear about which tycoon has bought which building from another prominent person who is broke and has left the country. There is also no shortage of theories on how people become rich. They will show you a tall building in Kampala and then narrate to you how the owner smuggled narcotics to break into the ranks of millionaires. Or he had access to the Swiss account of a top army officer who used to purchase weapons for the country but died suddenly before surrendering the taxpayers' billions to the national treasury. Maybe the owner controlled a smuggling racket taking coltan from Congo to Germany. The people will always have a sinister explanation for origins of the big property owners' wealth. If you don't believe them, then you are not a Kampalan.

Lawyer

We are the learned brothers of Uganda. We are all found in Kampala, of course. What would we be doing upcountry where nobody can afford our services? Learned we are; but being brothers doesn't mean we have to be brotherly to everybody, including peasants.

We go through a lot to become advocates of the High Court. First of all, your grades at A level must be well above average if you are to be admitted to the faculty of law at Makerere University. But even then, not everybody who starts out for the law degree gets admitted to the bar. A good number fail. Those who get mere pass degrees are not admitted to the Law Development Centre, where pretty few of us qualify with the diploma to practise.

And that is not enough. To be a successful advocate, you need to work as a state attorney for some two years. Patiently, you survive on the ridiculously low pay and watch as defence lawyers make you look foolish because your employer, government, does not facilitate you to do a good job. Trial magistrates rebuke you several times a day because your witnesses, who include CID officers, fail to turn up. After being made to look like an ass for two years, you finally venture out into private practice, angry, broke, but wiser.

That period of humiliation we spend in government service is a worthwhile investment. The

suffering entitles us to enjoy the millions we make in private practice without guilt.

At first, you have to do with the cases of village rapists. They are really hopeless, these rapists. Some of them have been to prison for stealing chickens and removing side mirrors and indicator lights from parked cars. They do not even have the money. But when they are arrested for rape, their relatives realise they must have a lawyer because rape is a capital offence only triable by the High Court. So they scrounge around and bring a deposit of a few dollars to your slum office to open up a file. These rapists and defilers – that is anybody who has sex with a girl below the age of eighteen - have kept starting lawyers in business ever since the law made their offences punishable by death. But you don't want to be seen in court only representing such vermin. You only remain in these

51

undignified activities for as long as you must, until a real case comes up.

It may come in the form of a Congolese businessman whose gold has been stolen by a rich Ugandan. It could be a messy divorce involving a rich illiterate businessman. That is where the money is – from disputes involving rich people. And it gets you into the newspapers. Once you get there, there is no looking back. Foreign businessmen are especially good. Once you handle one well, he will refer his countrymen to you and you will represent all their interests – without having to go to court.

You go to court only if your client has a big claim against the government. Then you defeat the government – as expected, for a large settlement.

All those years of suffering while working for government pay off because you know all its weaknesses. Otherwise, court is really for beginners. A serious lawyer does most of his work in his air-conditioned office or at exclusive five star clubs. When things get tough, he can fly to Nairobi or London to have a word with the judge. We never bribe judges. But they are also human. When we get a chance to talk with them, we remind them of the insults that politicians heap on them day in day out. That tends to soften them and they begin to get inclined to seeing things our way.

So you see how far we really come from. It is a long way, from law school to a respected learned brother whose name keeps appearing in the papers, in glorious terms. So, do not begrudge us our wealth.

▰▰◖▰ NGO

Uganda must be having one of the highest NGO to population ratios in the world. We could even be talking of the NGOs per capita ratio, for there might be as many NGOs as there are people in this land. There are, for instance, far more NGOs for helping street children than there are actual kids on the streets. The ratio is over two NGOs per street kid.

The NGO epidemic started in the late eighties and by the mid-nineties, it had blown up into a full-fledged explosion that was truly out of control. Previously, non-governmental organisations were run by white foreigners and were known for paying their employees several times more than government workers.

Then someone discovered that Ugandans too could form NGOs, and our definition or perception of NGOs changed forever. Today, an NGO is a very small business with a very big name and a very large four-wheel-drive car driven by the founder who gets some wealthy foreign visitors once a year.

The road to NGO ownership is quite wide and almost anybody can become a proud director of one. Problem is, there are so many of them they have lost a lot of their weight. But that does not mean they do not pay the founders enough for a decent livelihood.

Here is how to set up a prosperous NGO: First look for the most appealing subject of the day and proceed to find the sexiest name for your NGO. A typical NGO name could be 'Grassroots Democratisation Mobilisation Activists', or 'The Support Network for Adversely Affected Volunteers of the HIV/AIDS Vaccination Trials'.

After doing the paperwork, go to one of the donor agencies and persuade them about your programme. Proclaim passionately how the masses are not aware of the issues at hand, or are at risk of a certain danger which you have perceived. Then go on to confidently show how your programme is the answer. All the time, make sure you use the appropriate language, throwing in words like 'sensitisation' and 'vulnerable groups'. Don't forget to refer to 'measurable outcomes' and 'periodic evaluation' while at it. Once they agree to fund one sensitisation workshop for you, you can declare your days of struggle over. Unless you are very careless, you have made your entry into the NGO world.

Arrange the sensitisation workshop as meticulously as possible; your future depends on it. Invite the ambassador of the country whose donor agency has funded the workshop to open it. At that stage, it pays to proclaim loudly how non-partisan you are. It will help bring in the local councillors to grace the opening ceremony. The local headteachers can also come in handy, bringing in school kids and teachers to fill the local hall.

But all this will be useless if you do not get media coverage. It may not be difficult to get crews from the one hundred radio stations broadcasting out of Kampala though the TV crews tend to be more expensive. But no pennies should be spared on this occasion. People need to see an ambassador on TV at your function if they are to take your NGO seriously.

After the successful launch workshop, prepare for the big one. The venue should be Makerere University or one of those halls built near cathedrals. Invite the most controversial politicians from both government and the opposition camps. Send the invitations to the media houses, with a list of the speakers. What you want is a big clash of well known public figures to make the front pages of the dailies and several minutes of radio and TV airtime. Journalists will be on the lookout for your subsequent seminars.

You crown your career as an NGO operator with several appearances on radio and TV talk shows. By now yours is a household name and your face in a newspaper can be recognised by an average adult of sound mind. You make several trips abroad to attend seminars and conferences. You open a few branches in the country but make sure you retain tight control over the finances. You can even finance a few councillors' election campaigns. Brother, Sister, you have been launched.

■○■ Sex worker

For centuries, our society has run a quiet sex industry that operated smoothly. Most adults were involved in it and the public authorities left it undisturbed because it wasn't being run in the public domain. That is until some clumsy young women decided to bring it out in the open on the street, giving out our national secrets and attracting the attention of the government, which had decided to ignore the sex business.

Before those silly girls you see lining the streets of Kampala at night came out, the city had a flourishing sex business, which was joined by scores of polite, nicely brought up and well educated young ladies every year. These dignified sex workers are hidden among the thousands of girls who come from high schools from all over the country and get fixed at the university campus of Makerere, the nurses' school on Mulago hill, the national college of commerce at Nakawa, other colleges like Kyambogo, several nursing colleges on the hills of Kampala and high schools in the city.

The hungry men of the city have a wide selection. Before the whole thing became so competitive and crowded, the middle-aged man from town would visit the campus to identify the girl who would pretend to be his girlfriend for the next three years. But after the market became hectic, the man does not have to search. It is the girls who do the

57

searching through their networks, which work as informal matchmaking agencies. After identifying the vulnerable man, an 'accidental' meeting is arranged and he pairs up with the girl whose client he will be for the next three years as she pursues her degree course.

It is a near-perfect relationship, with him providing her with both necessities and luxuries and she making him comfortable once in a while. Her campus room becomes a cosy nest lined with the latest electronics, she gets to wear clothes and shoes ordinary working women can't afford and her mobile phone never runs out of airtime credit. She stops bothering her parents frequently for cash and necessities. When her campus-based boyfriend visits, he is told of the generous uncle who bought the latest DVD set. He is not fooled about the 'uncle', but accepts quietly, knowing that the girl keeps three men in her life. Himself, because he helps her with the hard studies and does all her coursework assignments, the 'uncle' who provides the cash and goodies, and the genuine boyfriend whom she hopes to marry one day. The first two are in reality clients, and they know that their tenure will be up some day.

The money spewing 'uncle' will leave her life after funding her graduation party on completion of her course. He cannot afford to keep her moving around town freely while still in liaison with him – his wife might find out about her. He has to replace her with a new college entrant and start the three-

year transaction all over again. The academic
boyfriend also knows he will be of no use to the girl
after she has sat her last exam, and both of them enter
the job market, knocking on unfriendly office doors.

These transactions have been going on for ages,
and there was hardly any need for an open sex
market. Men of all social and financial ranks could
find someone with whom to exchange their money
for temporary affection without the crass haggling
over prices. Taxi drivers and conductors are mostly
clients of girls in city day high schools. The girls
travel free in the public commuter minibuses all
over the city. Their driver clients even show them
to other drivers with strict instructions that they
are not to pay any fare for their journeys.

The girls who advance in education shed their
lowly clients in the process. The taxi drivers,

shopkeepers and such clients also replace the girls and become clients to new ones. The girls who do not continue with higher studies get some form of terminal benefits from the clients in the form of capital to set up a small beauty salon, kiosk or small shop. They may however have to earn the retirement package by producing a baby for the client. For this, a 'pension' in the form of monthly rent for one or two years may be added to the package.

A Ugandan sexual client has always been a gentleman, and a very polite one at that. There are other loveless sexual transactions which start in bars and night clubs and end up in a 'lodge' next door a couple of hours later. But even these are transacted in a friendly atmosphere where the two pretend to be a loving couple, share drinks – bought by the man of course – and whisper sweet nothings to each other before, during and for a while after the transaction.

Even the direct commercial transactions were always restricted to two or three designated slums of Kampala. The busiest was Kisenyi which is near the bus terminals and serve travellers. Katanga, located near the university, served mostly medical students as it lies between the main campus and the teaching hospital of Mulago. Being busy men, the medical students usually have no time to pretend to be in love. There was also Makerere-Kivulu to serve other students and the general riffraff of the city.

These and other arrangements have ensured a sufficient supply of non-committal sex for Kampala's men for close to a century, and there was really no justifiable need for the open sex market in Kampala that started in the last decade of the 20th century. Those girls who parade the city streets at night flagging down strangers' cars have taken away the dignity that careful pretence had lent to Uganda's version of the oldest profession. A couple of years to the close of the last century, a woman cabinet minister even proposed to legalise the profession and have it taxed. She was silenced and the undignified offshoot of an ages-old activity goes on, at ridiculously low prices. Maybe the taxation idea should have been accepted, just to make it a bit expensive and cause people to respect sex.

Fortunately, however, the anti-AIDS campaign has been largely successful, with the sex workers embracing the condom like their life depends on it; and indeed it does. They ushered in the new millennium in style – by getting a million perfumed condoms to launch the innovation which they now use to serve their Kampala customers. May their trade remain as safe as can be!

▰ ● Professor

"What use is a professor who has nothing to profess?" Okot p'Bitek demanded angrily. The renowned Ugandan writer was delivering a public lecture in a filled-to-overflowing main hall of Makerere University, one hot afternoon in 1981. But there were no professors in the audience to answer his question. We were busy elsewhere in the city, looking for money in different non-intellectual pursuits in order to make our personal budgets balance. It was undergraduates who later told us the story.

The hall was full of undergraduates and ordinary members of the public eager to hear from the writer, who had just returned from exile. Okot p'Bitek had returned to find a very different Makerere from the one he had left in the sixties when it was still the continental centre of academic excellence, fondly referred to as the Oxford of Africa.

A couple of years after Okot p'Bitek's public query, another Ugandan colleague of ours who tried to profess was stripped of his citizenship. Professor Mahmood Mamdani had tried too early to exercise intellectual freedom and the government was not amused. However, the price Mamdani paid for intellectual honesty was not the steepest.

In the seventies, many of our colleagues had paid with their lives for expressing their opinions freely. Our other friends like Prof. Ali Mazrui (born Kenyan

but intellectually matured at Makerere) fled Kampala before the dictators exacted the ultimate price from them. By the mid-seventies, the intellectual desertification of Makerere was almost complete. Those of us who remained in the country had to play dumb in order to stay alive. We even went and sewed a beautiful gown, dressed up Field Marshal Idi Amin Dada, Life President of Uganda, and awarded him a PhD in Law. From then on, we addressed him reverently as Dr Amin, a title he loved so much that it prompted him to pay a visit to his 'fellow' doctors at the teaching hospital of Mulago. Once the staff meeting got under way, he asked the Minister of Health, who was a layman, to step out so that only 'doctors' remained in the room to discuss their own matters freely. "Fellow doctors," he began his address.

It was not only our fear for that eroded the once-excellent seat of knowledge. The economic destruction made scientific research an impossible luxury. Thus the Mulago medical school which had contributed a lot to the development of tropical medicine also went to sleep. The national referral hospital became crowded as the only place where Kampala's poor flocked to report all their first complaints – because it was a free government facility. Many of our medical colleagues simply left in disgust to go and work abroad. Many of those who remained were killed by the military regime.

By the middle of the seventies, we had come to the grim conclusion that a dead professor is no good. Those of us who remained in the country perfected the art of survival. Rule Number One was to keep your mouth shut; someone could be tempted to feed you with a bullet. However provocative or interesting way a discussion that came up in your presence, you had to keep quiet and avoid provoking the State's self-styled surgeons who had become obsessed with separating people's heads from their necks.

Rule Number Two was to stick to what is already written and published. As long as you were teaching, you had to avoid sounding original and only quote the over-quoted scholars of yesteryear. What with the classroom being infested with state secret agents who had to report to their headquarters which lecturer was teaching subversive ideas! That is how the famous yellow notes emerged. As a perfect don you kept your lecture notes of last year, which had not caused you any trouble and read the very same notes to this year's class. Over the years, the notes, which had originally been written on white paper, started turning yellowish-brown with age.

But it was not only the quest for safety that turned us into 'yellow-note professors'. The yellow notes were mainly a by-product of the double-digit inflation, which set in after the declaration of the economic war in 1972 that resulted in the collapse of the economy. Our salaries soon became meaningless and in order to survive, we had to engage in other income-generating activities, leaving us with no time to prepare for our classes, hence our resorting to using old notes.

The most honourable income-generating activity outside the lecture room was to continue teaching, albeit at a lower level. Soon the university dons were teaching in high schools, secondary schools and as the economic pressures increased, some even went down to 'lecture' in primary schools. That explains the emergence of several schools around Makerere hill – the manpower was readily available. You can envy or pity some Ugandan kids for being taught by professors right from nursery school through university.

The days of gun rule did not only send professors to teach in primary schools. To keep the family fed and somehow clothed, some of our colleagues ended up doing more interesting jobs. If you didn't want to teach, you converted your family saloon car into a cab and became a taxi driver. That is how our once distinguished professors ended up spending most of their time at the taxi stages, calling passengers and plying the city routes. Fortunately, there was a shortage of vehicles in Kampala and business was brisk. But unfortunately, sometimes you had to abandon brisk business to rush back to campus, pull the yellow notes from the dashboard and deliver lectures to your students.

Yet another option was to become a shopkeeper, dusting maize flour off your clothes and yellow notes from time to time to go and attend to your classes. Another industry that arose out of the situation was chicken rearing at home. Many garages in professors' homes became poultry farms. Other productive units developed in our homesteads, with our wives becoming local confectioners, frying cassava and pancakes to sell in student canteens that were mushrooming all over the campus. The era of military rule thus succeeded in removing most of the dignity usually associated with professors. But it taught us creative survival, as the period after has shown.

And finally the post-1986 era ushered in the new don. First, the new government took away as many of our colleagues as it could absorb and gave them comfortable jobs. Those of us whom the government did not want decided to design modern cash-spinning methods. The most popular, in which every lecturer is free to partake, are the evening classes. The 90s university education boom ensured there are more students than the staff can handle. What used to be an elite community of a few students paid for by the government gave way to self-sponsored students, multiplying the student population ten times. Since the nineties when Makerere introduced the evening classes, mostly populated by working people who want to add a degree to their CV, what matters most to us are the student numbers.

The more creative method of making money is to set up an NGO. Every other lecturer is attached to some NGO or other. We are behind the mushrooming of NGOs across the land. When you meet a Ugandan at a seminar in a foreign city advocating passionately for some rare bird species or fighting against the marginalisation of girls aged 15 to 16 years, chances are he is a full-time university lecturer and an NGO person on the side.

Whichever path we take to make some money, it demands so much of our time that commitment to excellence, for which the university was set up, is always sacrificed. So even in this computer age, the yellow notes are not about to go away.

■ ○ ■ President

Other than probably Yoweri Museveni, the other Ugandan presidents found it relatively easy to assume the country's highest office. Being a president in Uganda is many times about making promises. You enter office promising the citizens a paradise of sorts and by the end of your tenure, which may range from two months to two decades, you are giving explanations why you did not deliver on the lofty promises.

The first president was the king of Buganda, the central region from which the country's name is derived. Shortly after we got independence on October 9, 1962, Kabaka Edward Mutesa, 'King Freddie', became president of the entire Uganda. His own kingdom was at the height of its glory. Favourable world coffee prices ensured that his peasants could buy motorcycles and cars as well as send their children to good schools. His dream was to raise the whole of Uganda to Buganda's status, and he even donated his presidential salary for the development of Karamoja, that region where the colonialists did not want to disturb nature as they laid infrastructure in other parts of the country. Mutesa had true royal tastes, spending some time shooting elephants in the wilderness, attending parties and visiting other royals. By the way, he was a full colonel in the Queen's grenadier guards. A head of state serving in a foreign army? Royal

matters can be confusing. But Mutesa did not pay much attention to the structural contradictions of the system, which made him president but left him practically powerless. Even Premier Milton Obote didn't like that royal stuff too much. So in May 1966, he overthrew the king-cum-president, sending him to die in exile.

So Obote became our second president. He promised equality to all men and spent a lot of time castigating Baganda royals for their 'accident of birth'. He wrote something called the Common Man's Charter, and promised heaven to the common man. His habits were more working class – using both his hands. He often used one hand to hold a glass, and the other to hold the microphone and deliver brilliant speeches. His sparkling speeches often dwelt on how to deliver equality by conquering nobility in Buganda and the rest of the country. Occasionally, there was a variation: the hand that held the glass would carry the cigarette. Like a working class person he was, items travelled from his hand to his mouth.

But the paradise promised did not come. Prisons were filled with untried detainees. The country was under emergency rule to the very last day of his rule January 25, 1971, when Major General Idi Amin overthrew Obote.

Amin came with an 18-point document, explaining why he had taken the action 'to save a bad situation from getting worse'. He promised freedom and went ahead to ban politics, whatever that meant. He alone had the interpretation. Overnight he became a full general and soon after, a Field Marshal. He promised to enrich all black Ugandans and chased away all the Asians in what he called "The Economic War". (Victims of his 1972 expulsion eventually formed the new wealthy class in Britain, introducing corner shops and popularising Indian food in Europe.) Amin simply liked everything, without discrimination. Women, cars, power and more power. After he had taken all the titles there were in Uganda like Chancellor of Makerere University, Father of Twins and Sportsman Number One, he added a few British titles, in his version, including CBE – Conqueror of the British Empire. He was chased away in April 1979. By the way, Life President was one of his titles.

Amin was truly a unique president. He is the only one who cannot be accused of discrimination by favouring any group of Ugandans against others – everybody suffered under his rule. He used foreigners from Southern Sudan to keep the Ugandans cowed. But in a way he came close to fulfilling his promises. At the end of his eight-year rule in 1979, the economy was no longer poor – it was dead. The bad political system he found in 1971 was also gone. There was no system any more. He also brought equality to all Ugandans, for there was no gap between the rich and the poor – everybody became poor. Disunity was also gone. All the Ugandans were solidly united against him.

With the help of the Tanzanians, Idi Amin was dislodged and a university professor, by the name of Yusuf Lule, was appointed. He was carried to power by the Tanzanian army and Ugandan exile forces. Lule promised Ugandans heaven on earth. In his case, heaven was a return to the orderly society of the colonial era. He re-divided the country into four regions so people could be developed in their natural setting. He even had a nearly white inspector general of police; it felt like getting closer to the British way of doing things. The good old Uganda of the fifties would soon be back, the nostalgic Ugandans were reassured.

But before most Ugandans could learn to identify his face, the 68-year-old teacher was overthrown after 68 days in power. Before he could articulate his glorious promises more clearly, he was put on a plane to exile, and was kept firmly out until his death a few years later.

In came a lawyer, Godfrey Binaisa, QC. (Maybe the Queens of England one day will stop bestowing titles and ranks upon our presidents!) He was handed power on a silver platter during a caucus meeting of the ruling UNLF (Uganda National Liberation Front). Binaisa had a very big head, literally. He was proud of it. It contained a very big brain and he confused fellow politicians while amusing the public all the way. His promises were big time: A large aircraft factory in Western Uganda, petroleum exploitation ("My spineless predecessors were too timid and succumbed to foreign pressures not to mine our oil; I shall exploit it and we shall all be happy!") After eleven months, fellow politicians got tired and threw him out. Actually, they threw him in. He was the first serving head of state to be placed under arrest. All the others took off in time when overthrown. Binaisa was already a prisoner while he was still the president, and in a long transition that took several days, a strongman called Paulo Muwanga took over. That was in mid-1980.

Still following our story? Now Muwanga was another type altogether. He was a jack of all trades besides being a de facto Head of State. He did other things too, like running small shops, a transport business, farming, part-time soldiering, diplomacy, printing and publishing and real estate management. A businessman all the way, Muwanga organised an election, disregarded the poll results and gave the presidency to the highest bidder. In return, he was made Vice President and Minister of Defence. By the way, the highest bidder was Milton Obote, if you remember the name.

Obote was back for the second time. In his campaign talk, he kept saying that he had come back to start from where he had left off (in 1971) and complete the task (of fulfilling his promises to develop Uganda) that had been rudely interrupted (by Idi Amin's coup). He vowed to complete his party's unfinished business, and the nation waited in anticipation. The unfinished business turned out to be a ruthless campaign to quash the rebellions that cropped up all over the country. But even that he failed to finish, and his regime crumbled in July 1985 when General Tito Okello overthrew him.

As Obote was fleeing across the border, his VP, seasoned businessman Muwanga was made Prime Minister by the people who had overthrown the government in which he had been Defence Minister. Poor Maj. General Tito Okello Lutwa also made his promises. He spent the entire duration of his presidency in peace talks chaired by the Kenyan president in Nairobi. Okello promised to restore peace but total anarchy ensued instead. His Acholi people also never realised the dream he had inspired – of finally controlling Uganda. They had all along under the two Obote regimes only served as despised soldiers. But 'their' government only lasted six months.

The guerrilla force that had been fighting the second Obote government for five years ignored Okello's regime and continued its long march to

Kampala, taking power in January 1986. The leader of the National Resistance Army guerrillas, Yoweri Museveni, took charge of the country. Museveni came in with his 10-point programme which he had put together during the bush days. The document which was regugitated continuously by his cadres, bore the hall-marks of the Communist Party manifesto with the central theme of building an "independent, integrated and self-sustaining economy". He strengthened ties with communist Cuba, North Korea and China and signed barter trade deals with them.

Instead of the economy getting better, it got worse, and Museveni quickly switched ideological sides, and became a fervent believer in the market economy. He sold off all government-owned companies and completely liberalised the econmy. Within six years of his taking power, the once laughable Uganda shilling became a fully convertible currency.

Although Museveni has not named any street or public facility after himself, he has stamped his personality on all aspects of Uganda's public life. He made all local and national administrative posts elective and taught the civilians including Catholic nuns how to operate sub-machine-guns.

Although Uganda is still dogged by instability in the north, Museveni restored stability, regular governance and pride to a country that had been shattered by two decades of instability. However, he still has some three years in power, and as the saying goes, even a week is a long time in politics.